I Want to Learn
al-Ikhlaas al-Falaq an-Nas

Written by Umm Bilaal Bint Sabir
Content Review @utrujjah_press
Cover Formatting @ilm.cards
Proofreading Umm AbdurRahmaan S. Bint Ahmed and Umm Yunus
Typesetting by Umm Bilaal Bint Sabir

2023 Al Huroof Publishing
© alhuroof
First Published August 2024

ISBN 978-1-917065-21-4

All enquiries to: alhuroof@hotmail.com
@al.huroof

Al Huroof Publishing

Learning my 1st Short Surahs

This book belongs to:

Dedicated to Ahsan,
Allaah yarhamhu, a special boy who taught
the author the last two surahs of the Qur'aan,
in his short but blessed life.

May Allaah Subhanahu, increase his
reward of sadaqa jariyah ameen.

بِسْمِ اللَّه

All Praise is for Allaah the Lord of the whole of creation and may Allaah extol and grant peace and security to our Prophet Muhammad (sallAllaahu 'alayhi wa sallam), and to his true followers and to his companions (radhiAllaahu 'anhum), all of them.
To Proceed:

How to Use this Book

Learning to read the short surahs is a special time for any young Muslim who is beginning their journey of memorising the Qur'aan.

Learning, memorising and understanding the Qur'aan can be difficult all at once. Understanding the meaning can be even more difficult for those who do not know the Arabic language.

This book has been designed as a helping guide for English Speakers who would like to understand the meaning of the last three surahs in English; as they are learning them. An ayah by ayah translation of the meaning* has been given followed by the complete surah at the end.
The explanation (tafseer) of the ayah has also been included.
*The Qur'aan cannot be translated only the meaning can be translated.

References

The translation has been taken from The Noble Qur'aan, Darussalaam by Dr. Muhammad Hilali and Dr.Muhsin Khan. Tafsīrāt of these suwar have been taken from At-Tabari, Imam as Sa'di, Sahih al-Bukhari and others; explained by Shaykh Uthaymeen rahimahullaah and Shaykh Fawzaan hafidhahullaah.

About Al Huroof

Al Huroof is a small project aimed at producing authentic Islamic teaching aids and material. These are based on the Qur'aan and Sunnah, with the understanding of the Prophet Muhammad (sallAllaahu 'alayhi wa sallam), and his righteous companions - Salaf-us-Saalih - (radhiAllaahu 'anhum). After thanking Allaah, Subhaanahu, we would like to thank all those who have aided in this book, from formatting, checking and feedback.

May Allaah accept it as sadaqa jaariyah from us, ameen.

I want to learn

Surah
al-Ikhlaas
al-Falaq
an-Nas

How do I start?

Let's go over some basic Arabic vowels that you will need for these suwar.

Each ayah (verse) has been divided word by word. When you see this little sign it means 'Iqra' (read or recite).

Tafsīrāt of these suwar have been taken from At-Tabari, Imam as Sa'di, Sahih al-Bukhari and others; and explained by Shyakh Uthaymeen rahimahullaah and Shaykh Fawzaan hafidhahullaah.

اقرأ

Basic Vowels

Dhamma

tu   bu   'u

Kasrah

ti   bi   ii

Fathah

ta   ba   a

Shaddah

ab-bu   ab-bi   ab-ba

Sukoon

ub   ib   ab

Dhammatayn

bunn   unn

Kasrahtayn

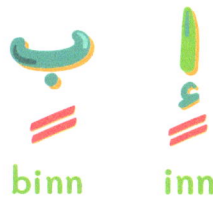

binn   inn

Fatahtayn

bann   ann

Lam - alif

laa

Hamza-alif

'u   'i   'a

Madd

4 or 6 counts

Dagger Alif

This is a long 'a' sound

Hamza-tul Wasl

This sound is not said if connecting with a previous word.

7

In the name of Allaah

We say bismillaah before we recite the Quraan. We also say it before we do something so that we can get Allaah's help and blessings in what we do. Saying bismillaah means we are calling upon all the names of Allaah.

بِسْمِ اللّٰهِ

اقرأ

The Most Merciful

This is one of the beautiful names of Allaah.
It means 'Rahma' which is mercy.
Allaah has a vast amount of Mercy and is the Most Merciful to all of His creation. We receive His Mercy everyday in so many ways.

الرَّحْمٰنِ

The Ever-Merciful

This is another one of the beautiful names of Allaah.

It means He is more Merciful, and gives special Mercy to those who believe in Him, those who follow His Prophets; and His Messengers and are Muslims.

الرّحِيمِ

اقرأ

now say it together

In the name of Allaah,
The Most Merciful,
The Ever-Merciful.

بِسْمِ اللّٰهِ الرَّحْمٰنِ الرَّحِيمِ

اقرأ

Say He is Allaah (who is) One

The non-believers or Jews asked the Prophet (sallAllaahu 'alayhi wa sallam) to describe his God and what He is made of! So Allaah revealed this surah for the Prophet (sallAllaahu 'alayhi wa sallam) and all Muslims to say.

Allaah is The One.
He is Unique in His Glory.

He is the Almighty and the Only One.

He has no partner and there is no one like Him.

Musnad Ahmad, Ibn Kathir,
Tirmidhi Tafsir

قُلْ هُوَ ٱللَّهُ أَحَدٌ

اقْرَأْ

Allaah is the Self-Sufficient

As-Samad is the Perfect Lord and Master.*He is the One who all His creatures need and are dependent on.

The One Who remains and never dies, the One Who neither eats nor drinks; free of all needs.

As-Samad means He is Complete in His Knowledge, Patience, Might and Ability.**

He is The One who is not in need of His creatures.

*The Ninety-Nine Names of Allaah – Dawud Burbank

**Al-'Aqidah Al-Wasitiyyah (2 Vol. Set) – Author:Shaykh Muhammad bin Salih Al-'Uthaimin – Publisher: Darussalam Publishers & Distributors

ٱللَّهُ ٱلصَّمَدُ

He does not (beget) have children...

To beget means to have a child.
To have a child means you have a partner.

Allaah is free from this.
He does not beget because there
is no one like Him.
Allaah, the Almighty, the Glorious
has no need of a child or a partner.

How could He have a son
or partner when He created
everything?*

*Surah Al An'am ayat 101

*The Ninety-Nine Names of Allaah – Dawud Burbank

**Al-'Aqidah Al-Wasitiyyah (2 Vol. Set) –
Author:Shaykh Muhammad bin Salih Al-'Uthaimin –
Publisher: Darussalam Publishers & Distributors

لَمْ يَلِدْ

اقرأ

nor is He born

Allaah is the First.
There was nothing before Him.*

He created everything.
Nothing was before Him.

He created everything.
How could He be born?

The non-believers say angels are
the daughters of Allaah!

The Jews say Uzair is the son of Allaah!

The Christians say Jesus is
the son of Allaah!**

None of them are true!

*The Ninety-Nine Names of Allaah – Dawud Burbank

**Surah Maryam ayah 88

وَلَمْ يُولَدْ

now say it together

He does not (beget)
have children,
nor is He born.

لَمْ يَلِدْ
وَلَمْ يُولَدْ

اقْرَأ

nor is there to Him anyone equal

There is no one equal to Him in His qualities.

Allaah denies that He begets or is born or that anything is equal to Him.

وَلَمْ يَكُن لَّهُ كُفُوًا أَحَدٌ

اقرأ

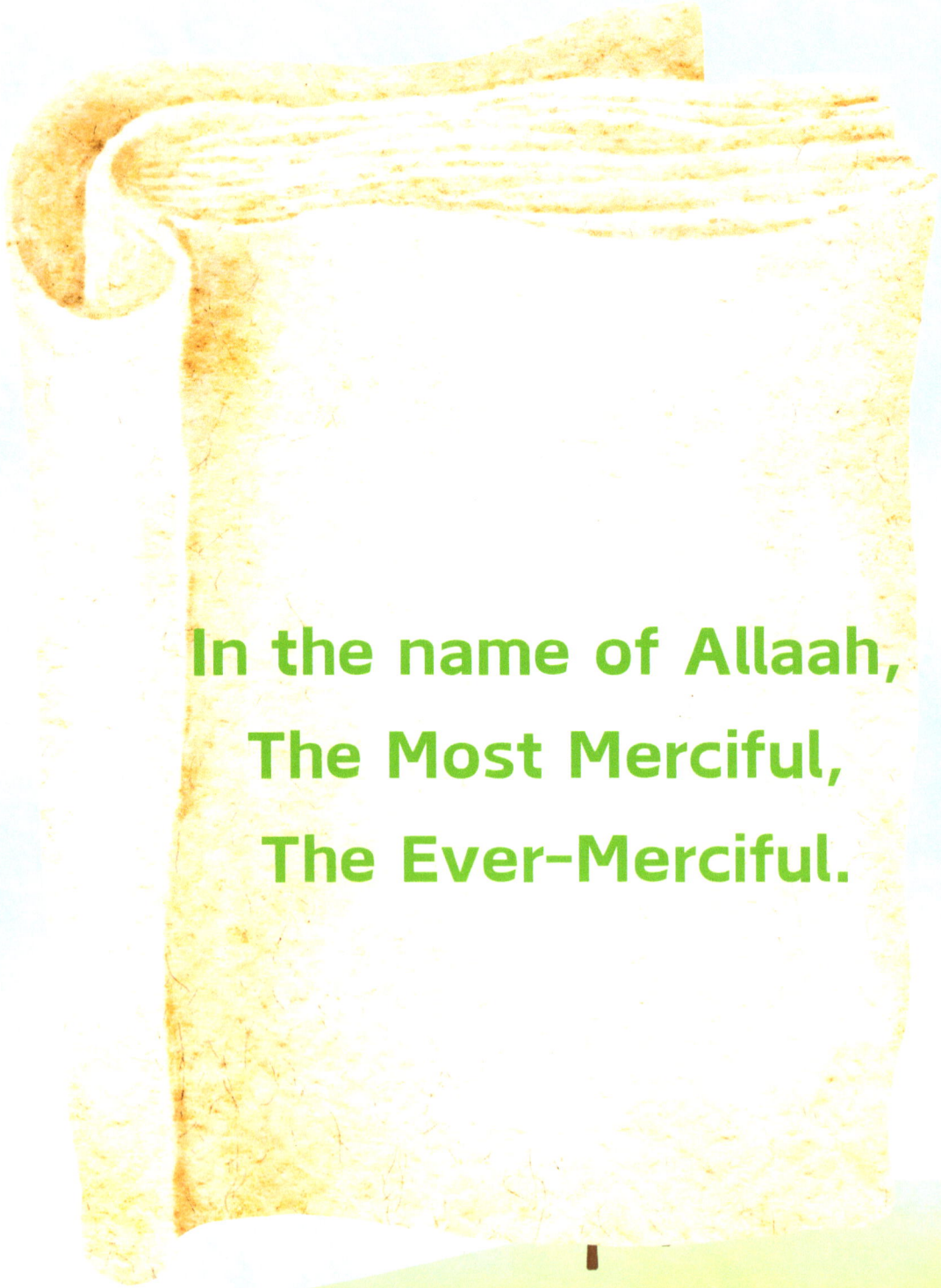

In the name of Allaah,
The Most Merciful,
The Ever-Merciful.

بِسْمِ اللّٰهِ الرَّحْمٰنِ الرَّحِيمِ

اقرأ

Say: I seek refuge with the Lord of the daybreak.

The Lord of the daybreak and dawn is Allaah. Allaah brings out the dawn and everything else that grows, like grains and fruit seeds that sprout*

Surah Al-An'am ayah 96

قُلْ أَعُوذُ بِرَبِّ ٱلْفَلَقِ

اقرأ

From the evil of what He has created.

This includes the evil of the creatures and the evil of ourselves. Why ourselves? Because we are part of the creation and our souls are created weak. We can go towards things that are wrong. So we seek refuge from our own souls first.*

We also seek refuge from theshaytaan, jinns, animals and everything else in the creation.

Khutabbal al Hajjar

32

مِن شَرِّ مَا خَلَقَ

اقرأ

33

And from the evil of the night when it grows dark.

This means when the night enters with its darkness it becomes Ghaasiq.* This is when wild animals and beasts come out. It also means when the moon brightens with its light. It is also Ghaasiq** because it only happens at night.

Allaah created the darkness, the night and everything in it and we seek refuge from the evil of it all.

Sunan al-Tirmidhī 3366

*Surah Al-Isra ayah 78

وَمِن شَرِّ غَاسِقٍ إِذَا وَقَبَ

اقرأ

And from the evil of those who blow in the knots.

These are the evil witches who tie knots and make spells and call the names of the shayateen when they blow onto the knots. They tie and blow, tie and blow, tie and blow.

They are wicked men or women who want to harm other people.

Allaah is the Only One to protect us.

وَمِن شَرِّ ٱلنَّفَّٰثَٰتِ فِي ٱلْعُقَدِ

اقرأ

37

And from the evil of the envier when he envies

The envier is one who does not like to see people have the blessings of Allaah.

They are upset to see what Allaah gives to others like money, honour, knowledge or even a nice car.

This is the evil eye. When a person or their things are harmed by others.

وَمِن شَرِّ حَاسِدٍ إِذَا حَسَدَ

اقرأ

39

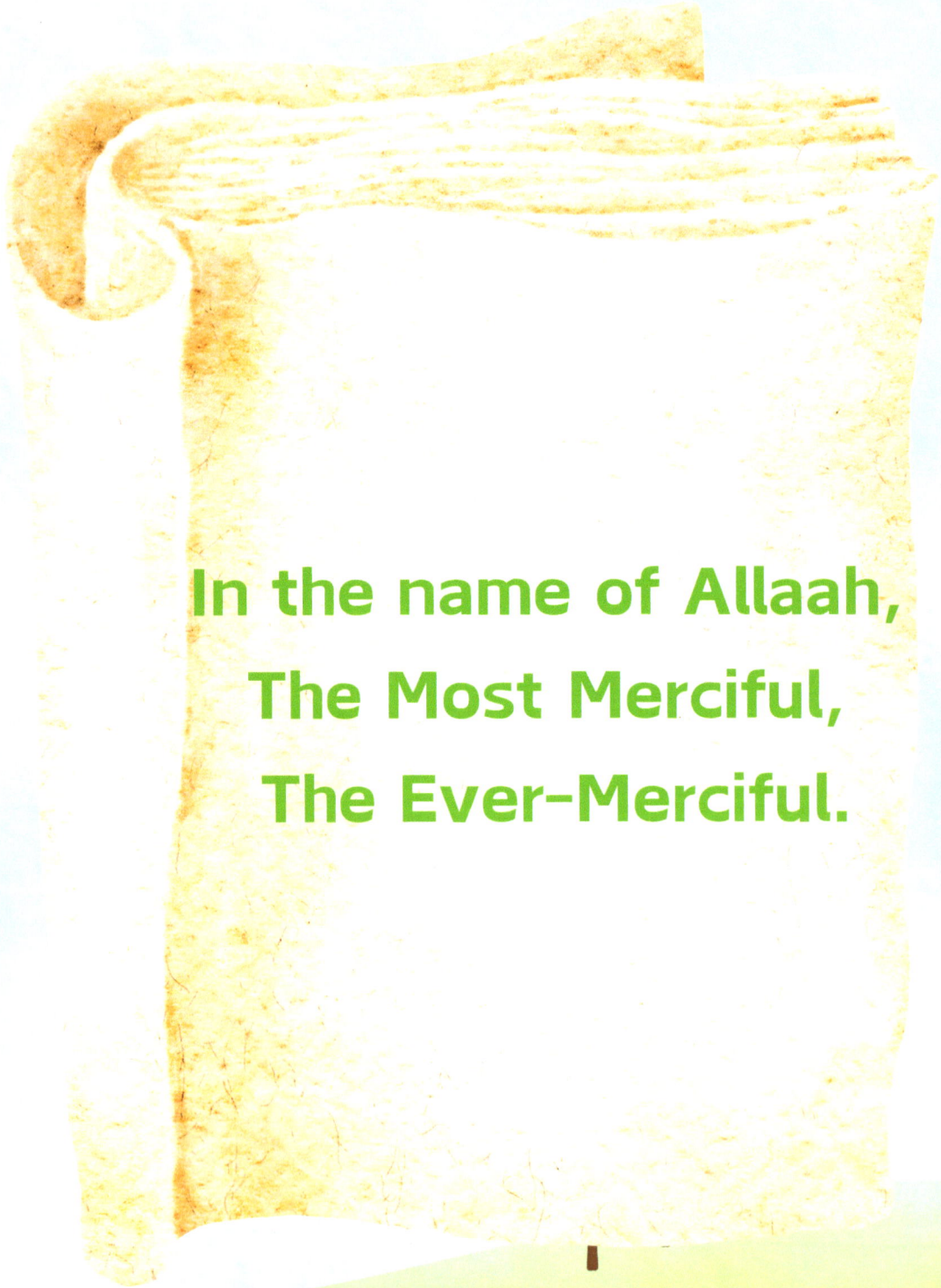

In the name of Allaah,
The Most Merciful,
The Ever-Merciful.

بِسْمِ اللَّهِ أَلرَّحْمَٰنِ الرَّحِيمِ

اقرأ

Say: I seek refuge...

Allaah is telling the Prophet (sallAllaahu 'alayhi wa salaam), and mankind to seek safety and refuge or shelter with...

قُلْ أَعُوذُ

with the Lord of mankind.

Ar-Rabb is the Lord, who takes care of His slaves through His blessings on them. He guides them, gives them knowledge, provides for them and controls everything.

Ar-Rabb is the Lord of all the people, the angels and the jinn, the skies, the earth, the sun, the moon and all that exists.

Here Allaah only mentions people.

بِرَبِّ النَّاسِ

اقرأ

now say it together

Say: I seek refuge with the Lord of mankind.

قُلْ أَعُوذُ بِرَبِّ النَّاسِ

47

The King of mankind

The King of mankind who is the only One with the Almighty Power and Complete ownership over people. He is Allaah, the Almighty.

Allaah gives power to whom He wills, and takes it away from whom He wills, honours whom He wills and degrades whom He wills ...*

SUrah Al-'Imran ayah 26

مَلِكِ ٱلنَّاسِ

اقرأ

49

The Ilaah of mankind,

The Ilaah of mankind means
He is the Almighty, the Only
one to be worshipped.

And the Only One to be
worshipped and praised in
the hearts is Allaah,
The Mighty.

إِلَهِ ٱلنَّاسِ

اقرأ

From the evil of the whisperer who withdraws

The whispers from shaytaan are ideas or thoughts that are not real.

Al-Khannas is the shaytaan who runs when the person remembers Allaah, and returns when they forget about Allaah.

He runs away so fast when he hears the athan and is so sad to hear the name of Allaah!

مِن شَرِّ ٱلْوَسْوَاسِ ٱلْخَنَّاسِ

اقرأ

Who whispers in the breasts of mankind.

When shaytaan whispers into the hearts of people we should quickly turn to Allaah, the Perfect, the Most High.

Only by remembering Allaah can we be safe from these whispers.

ٱلَّذِى
يُوَسْوِسُ
فِى صُدُورِ
ٱلنَّاسِ

from the jinn and mankind

This means that the whispers from the jinn or mankind.

The whispers of jinn are well known, because they flow in people like blood in the veins.

The whispers are from people who come with evil thoughts or ideas and make them look beautiful – until you follow them!
We ask Allaah to protect us.

مِنَ الْجِنَّةِ
وَالنَّاسِ

اقرأ

57

When you are ready you can try and recite the suwar together!

سُورَةُ الْإِخْلَاصِ

بِسْمِ ٱللَّهِ ٱلرَّحْمَٰنِ ٱلرَّحِيمِ

قُلْ هُوَ ٱللَّهُ أَحَدٌ ﴿١﴾ ٱللَّهُ ٱلصَّمَدُ ﴿٢﴾

لَمْ يَلِدْ وَلَمْ يُولَدْ ﴿٣﴾ وَلَمْ يَكُن لَّهُ كُفُوًا أَحَدٌ ﴿٤﴾

سُورَةُ الْفَلَقِ

بِسْمِ ٱللَّهِ ٱلرَّحْمَٰنِ ٱلرَّحِيمِ

قُلْ أَعُوذُ بِرَبِّ ٱلْفَلَقِ ﴿١﴾

مِن شَرِّ مَا خَلَقَ ﴿٢﴾ وَمِن شَرِّ غَاسِقٍ إِذَا وَقَبَ ﴿٣﴾

وَمِن شَرِّ ٱلنَّفَّٰثَٰتِ فِى ٱلْعُقَدِ ﴿٤﴾ وَمِن شَرِّ حَاسِدٍ إِذَا حَسَدَ ﴿٥﴾

سُورَةُ النَّاسِ

بِسْمِ ٱللَّهِ ٱلرَّحْمَٰنِ ٱلرَّحِيمِ

قُلْ أَعُوذُ بِرَبِّ ٱلنَّاسِ ﴿١﴾ مَلِكِ ٱلنَّاسِ ﴿٢﴾

إِلَٰهِ ٱلنَّاسِ ﴿٣﴾ مِن شَرِّ ٱلْوَسْوَاسِ ٱلْخَنَّاسِ ﴿٤﴾

ٱلَّذِى يُوَسْوِسُ فِى صُدُورِ ٱلنَّاسِ ﴿٥﴾ مِنَ ٱلْجِنَّةِ وَٱلنَّاسِ

Learning my 1st Short Surahs

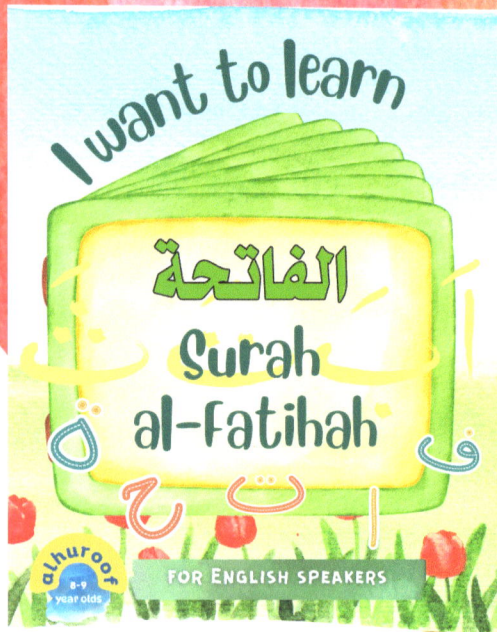

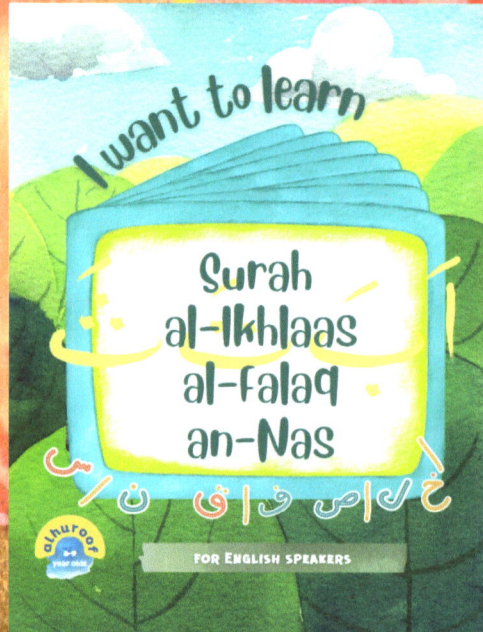

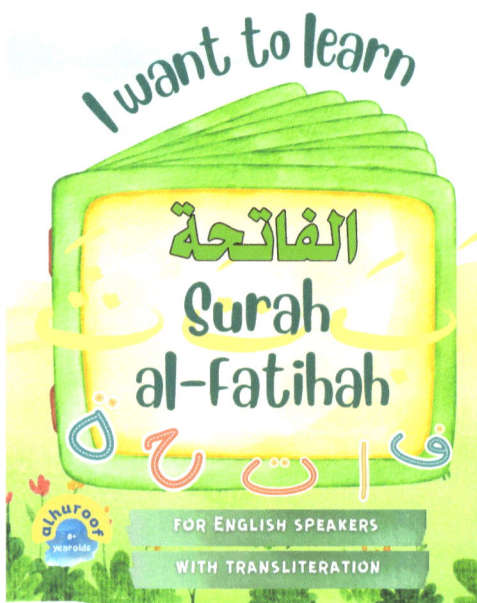

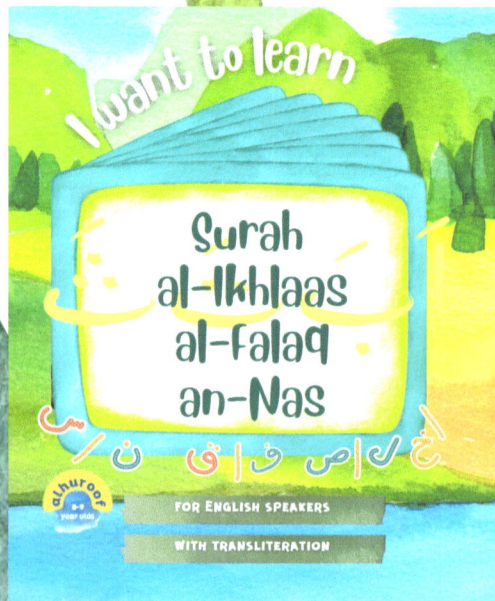

I want to learn

الفاتحة
Surah al-Fatihah

alhuroof
8-9 year olds

FOR ENGLISH SPEAKERS

I want to learn

Surah al-Ikhlaas al-Falaq an-Nas

alhuroof
8-9

FOR ENGLISH SPEAKERS

I want to learn

الفاتحة
Surah al-Fatihah

alhuroof
8+ year olds

FOR ENGLISH SPEAKERS

WITH TRANSLITERATION

I want to learn

Surah al-Ikhlaas al-Falaq an-Nas

alhuroof
8-9 year olds

FOR ENGLISH SPEAKERS

WITH TRANSLITERATION

designed for young
or new Muslims

Arabic and
Engish

meaning or
meaning with
transliteration

word by word
ayah by ayah
whole surah

Al Huroof Publishing

ا ب ت ث ج ح

خ د ذ ر ز س

ش ص ض ط ظ ع

غ ف ق ك ل م

ن و هـ ي

www.ingramcontent.com/pod-product-compliance
Lightning Source LLC
Chambersburg PA
CBHW042006080426
42733CB00003B/26